A Gift From:

_____

Car Detailing San Antonio

CAR DETAILING
SAN ANTONIO

Your Ultimate Guide to Finding and Selecting the Right Auto Detailer

DYLAN TYBURSKI

Car Detailing San Antonio:
Your Ultimate Guide to Finding and Selecting the Right Auto Detailer

ISBN: 978-0-9816557-2-7
Library of Congress Control Number: 2023944767

Copyright © 2023 Profit Inner Circle, LLC

All rights reserved. No part of this publication may be reproduced, stored in a retrieval system, or transmitted, in any form, or by any means, electronic, mechanical, recorded, photocopy, or otherwise, without the prior written permission of the copyright owner except by a reviewer who may quote brief passages in a review.

Although the publisher and the author have made every effort to ensure that the information in this book and its ancillary materials was correct at press time, and while this publication intends to provide accurate information in regard to the subject matter covered, neither the author nor publisher assumes any responsibility for errors, inaccuracies or omissions and is not responsible for any loss by the customer in any manner. Any slights of people or organizations are unintentional.

Published by:

Profit Inner Circle, LLC
PO Box 591296
San Antonio, TX 78259
www.ProfitInnerCircle.com

For more information on the author, visit www.AffluentAutoSpa.com.

Design by Imagine!® Studios
www.ArtsImagine.com

First printing: October 2023

Register Your Book Now!

Register your book so we can invite you to our client appreciation gatherings and keep you updated on our latest and greatest offerings.

Scan the QR code or go to AffluentAutoSpa.com/register

CONTENTS

Chapter 1
About the Author—Dylan Tyburski 1

Chapter 2
The Benefits of Auto Detailing 15

Chapter 3
Auto Detailing May Increase Your
Resale Value 23

Chapter 4
The Difference Between Car Washing
and Auto Detailing 27

Chapter 5
How a Do-it-Yourself Approach May
Damage Your Vehicle. 33

Chapter 6
Myth #1: Washing Your Vehicle When
it's Dirty is Good Enough 39

Chapter 7
IronX: The Secret Ingredient 47

Chapter 8
Advanced Clay Bar Treatment 53

Chapter 9
Paint Correction 57

Chapter 10
Surface Scratches 61

Chapter 11
Paint Swirls vs. No Paint Swirls 65

Chapter 12
Myth #2: Electric Machines are
Damaging to Your Vehicle's Paint. 71

Chapter 13
Myth #3: Polishing Isn't Important in
Keeping Your Paint Looking Like New 77

Chapter 14
What is Polishing and What are the
Various Methods?. .81

Chapter 15
What is Ceramic Coating and Why You
Should Have it Applied 85

Contents

Chapter 16
How Does Waxing Compare to Ceramic
Coating?............................89

Chapter 17
Ceramic Coating for Your Glass..........97

Chapter 18
What About Interior Detailing?..........101

Chapter 19
The Importance of the Right Training
and Education.......................105

Chapter 20
What is the Investment for High Quality
Detailing?..........................109

Chapter 21
The Benefits of Mobile Auto Detailing.....115

Chapter 22
Why Auto Enthusiasts Choose a
Detailing Maintenance Program.........121

Chapter 23
What Clients, Just Like You, are Saying
About the Affluent Auto Spa............129

Help us Build a "Thrive and Shine" Community!

This book wants to travel . . . after you read the book, please pass it along to your family, friends, and associates. (Please remember to write your information on the first line.)

Name	**City, State**	**Date**

Chapter 1

ABOUT THE AUTHOR— DYLAN TYBURSKI

ABOUT DYLAN

Ever since childhood, he has loved cars! From humble beginnings as a "car washer" to Founder of the Affluent Auto Spa, Dylan has always been passionate about cars, especially the "clean and fast" ones!

When Dylan was 16 years old and attending Ronald Reagan High School, he began his first part-time job as a car wash attendant at the Wash Tub. He assisted customers with their vehicles' interior and exterior cleaning (and detailing) and loved it!

About the Author—Dylan Tyburski

Three key lessons he carries with him today are the importance of ongoing improvement, delivering outstanding value, and providing a high-quality service. His passion for cars continued as he served as a valet attendant (and supervisor) at the JW Marriott San Antonio Hill Country Resort and Spa.

> **THREE KEY LESSONS HE CARRIES WITH HIM TODAY ARE THE IMPORTANCE OF ONGOING IMPROVEMENT, DELIVERING OUTSTANDING VALUE, AND PROVIDING A HIGH-QUALITY SERVICE.**

After obtaining his Construction Technology degree, he worked part-time for a local gutter installation company. Unfortunately (or fortunately for Dylan), during the 2020 CoronaVirus disease, the company experienced a reduction in force. So, Dylan made the bold entrepreneurial move to pursue his passion for detailing cars full-time and created the Affluent Auto Spa.

Dylan says, "This does not feel like work, I enjoy what I'm doing, and it's my passion!" The Affluent Auto Spa is one of the top-rated auto detailing companies in the San Antonio area.

ABOUT THE AFFLUENT AUTO SPA

Check out these selected Affluent Auto Spa vehicle transformations here:

AffluentAutoSpa.com/Gallery

About the Author—Dylan Tyburski

CHECK OUT THESE SELECTED AFFLUENT AUTO SPA VEHICLE TRANSFORMATIONS HERE:

AFFLUENTAUTOSPA.COM/ GALLERY

Difference Maker #1: Customized Treatment Plan

As soon as we arrive, we immediately create your customized "treatment plan" that ensures we deliver the highest quality outcome for your vehicle.

Difference Maker #2: Highest Quality "Lotions and Potions"

All of our cleaners, polishes, sealants, waxes, dressings, conditioners, compounds, degreasers, etc. are hand selected from top automotive detailing suppliers to ensure maximum shine, protection, durability, and depth of gloss.

Difference Maker #3: Photo and/or Video Updates Each Step of the Way

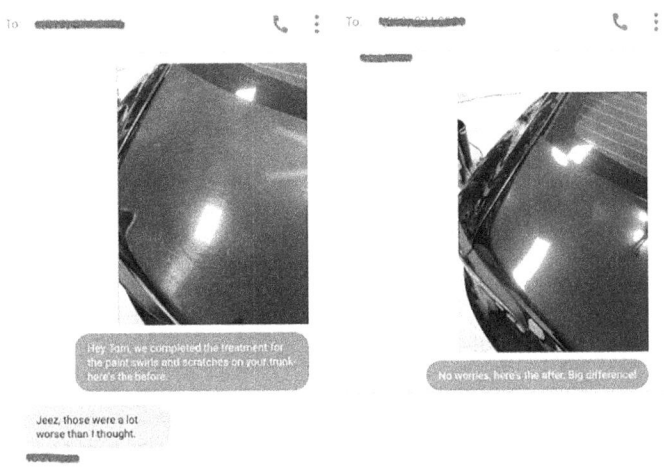

Rest assured, you'll know exactly what's being done, how it's being done, and the positive effects of the services being performed each step of the way. We even update you on our progress by providing you with photo and/or video updates throughout the day.

Like any other high-quality service you are accustomed to, we schedule personalized consultations. This is because not every vehicle needs a full-blown ceramic coating, and not every vehicle would look good enough after only a wash and vacuum. After we assess and diagnose your vehicle, we prescribe a customized treatment plan that delivers outstanding results!

Reserve Your Vehicle Consultation-Estimate Now. It's so Easy and Convenient Because We Come to You!

AffluentAutoSpa.com

Call/Text **(210) 679-1472**

Pickup/delivery service available for non-mobile treatments

Licensed + Insured

About the Author—Dylan Tyburski

We'll treat your vehicle right at your home! We proudly bring our professional mobile vehicle detailing in San Antonio services to your home. No need to find rides to or from our location, no more wondering how your vehicle is being taken care of, and most importantly, no more inconvenience! We'll treat your vehicle right at your home!

As soon as we arrive, we immediately create your customized "treatment plan" to ensure we deliver your vehicle's highest quality outcome. The Affluent Auto Spa is one of the area's top San Antonio mobile vehicle detailing companies.

The Affluent Auto Spa is NOT your "typical" auto detailing San Antonio shop because the others usually work like this: you drop off your vehicle and pick it up when it's ready. Sounds good so far, but have you ever wondered what is done while you are away? Have you ever pondered on what services were performed on your vehicle?

Rest assured, with Affluent Auto Spa, you'll know exactly what's being done, how it's being done, and the positive effects of the treatments being performed at each step. We even update you on our progress by providing you with photo and/or video updates throughout the treatment.

Let's have an open conversation about pricing. Because we get this question occasionally, let's cover it now. "Why are your prices higher than others for auto detailing?"

Our vehicle treatment plans are high quality and we deliver outstanding results. Therefore, our pricing (or your investment) for our treatment plans is often higher than "typical" San Antonio vehicle detailing shops.

We invest in the top training, education, and certifications to increase our team's knowledge, skills, and abilities. We also invest in the latest and greatest technology, "lotions and potions" and the most cutting-edge equipment available. This means that we provide you with the highest quality outcome for your vehicles. We are very proud of our people, processes, and technology and our clients agree that this is a good thing.

About the Author—Dylan Tyburski

Our vehicle treatment plans are not "cheap", no high-quality professional service is. If you are seeking a less expensive option or a cookie-cutter approach that is not customized for you, our business may not be right for you.

However, if you are looking for the right auto detailing San Antonio company that:

- Delivers customized treatment plans.
- Invests in the latest and greatest technology.
- Utilizes the top performing "lotions and potions" and the most cutting-edge equipment available.
- Invests in the ultimate training, education, and certifications to increase our team's knowledge, skills, and abilities.
- then the Affluent Auto Spa is right for you!

AffluentAutoSpa.com

What to expect (depending on the treatment plan you select):

- We wash your vehicle by hand twice utilizing a foam cannon combined with microfiber hand mitts and then we dry it with clean microfiber cloths. This ensures all dirt and dust are removed before polishing/waxing.

- *Important*—Then we apply iron remover. This step removes foreign substances from your paint including mineral deposits, road tar, tree sap, and airborne pollution.

- We perform mechanical decontamination using a clay barring treatment. This removes surface contaminants from everyday driving and restores the absolute smoothness of your paint.

- We ensure any bugs and tar are removed from your vehicle.

- Your paint surface imperfections are corrected or removed (not hidden with a glaze).

- Your plastics are protected from the sun's damaging rays.

- Your paint is polished to perfection by experienced professionals.

- Removes paint swirls and/or light scratches/scuffs, restores paint fading, and adds a gloss and shine to your paintwork.

- Your vehicle is hand waxed and will last for months. This adds an extra layer of protection against harsh weather, salt, bird droppings, tree sap, ultraviolet rays, and other assorted crud found in the air and on roads.

Special note: We often prescribe ceramic coatings because they provide an ultra-durable ceramic layer of protection sustaining that deep wet gloss while making your vehicle much easier to clean and maintain for years to come (ask about our lifetime guarantee!). It doesn't have any side-effects to the original paint and its long life span indirectly makes it very cost-effective for you as well.

In summary, our Ceramic Coating process:

- Provides protection from UV rays.
- Repels water, oils, dirt, and contaminants.
- Protects your vehicle from some scratches.
- Resists stains, bird droppings, water spots, and traffic film.
- and so much more!

At Affluent Auto Spa, we are passionate about delivering the best possible service to our clients. We understand that luxury and exotic vehicle owners have higher expectations when it comes to their vehicles, and we take great pride in meeting those expectations with our advanced detailing services.

Chapter 2

THE BENEFITS OF AUTO DETAILING

As a vehicle owner, it's important to maintain your vehicle in its best condition, both inside and out. Not only does a clean, well-maintained vehicle look aesthetically pleasing, but it also serves to protect your vehicle from the elements. This is where auto detailing comes in. Auto detailing is the process of cleaning, maintaining, and protecting your vehicle's exterior and interior.

Auto detailing is a great way to keep your vehicle looking its best and extend its life. Over time, dirt, grime, and wear and tear can make your vehicle look older than it is, but the right auto detailing can help restore it to its original condition. Detailing your vehicle can also be a cost-effective way to maintain your vehicle.

> **AUTO DETAILING IS A GREAT WAY TO KEEP YOUR VEHICLE LOOKING ITS BEST AND EXTEND ITS LIFE.**

The Benefits of Auto Detailing

Detailing includes a range of services that help restore your vehicle's paint, interior, and exterior. Detailing services can range from a basic wash and wax to more extensive services such as polishing, coating, and protecting your vehicle's surfaces.

Many higher-end auto detailing services also offer additional services such as:

- **Glass Treatment**—Provides you with clearer vision by repelling water off of the glass when you are driving.

- **Badge Removal**—This process removes auto emblems, logos, and other identifiers so you can give your vehicle a clean look and feel.

- **Headlight Restoration**—A headlight restoration service refinishes the light assembly back to clear lenses after they have been damaged by discoloration or yellowed by the sun and prolonged exposure to outside elements.

- **Carpet Deep Cleaning**—Odorless interior steam cleaning/shampooing treatment. This kills 99.99% of bacteria, removes even the toughest of mold growth (and prevents it from recurring), clears away trapped pollutants, eliminates dust mites, and removes stains, odors, grease, and bacteria.)

- **Stain Protectant**—Strong carpet protection blocks stains for easier cleanup because it penetrates into carpet fibers to lift out stains. It blocks stains so they don't set in.

- **Pet Hair Removal**—With advanced equipment, high-end detailers can even remove the toughest of your furry friend's hair from your interior.

The Benefits of Auto Detailing

Here are some of the benefits of auto detailing:

1. Protect your vehicle's exterior

Auto detailing helps to protect your vehicle's exterior by\ removing dirt, grime, and other contaminants that can damage your vehicle's paint. Professional detailing services use special cleaning solutions and polishes that help to restore the shine of your vehicle's paint and protect it from the elements. This can help to extend the life of your vehicle's paint and reduce the need for costly repairs.

2. Enhances your vehicle's appearance

Regular auto detailing can help to restore the shine of your vehicle's paint, making it look brand new. Professional detailing services can apply wax/sealants and other protectants to your vehicle's exterior to keep it looking its best. In addition, detailing services can also clean and sanitize your vehicle's interior, making it look and feel newer.

3. Improves resale value

Regular auto detailing can help to maximize the resale value of your vehicle. A well-maintained vehicle with a clean exterior and interior will attract more potential buyers, and you'll be able to get a higher price for it.

4. Helps to identify potential issues

During an auto detailing service, trained professionals are often able to spot potential issues with your vehicle. They can also recommend solutions to these problems, saving you time and money in the long run.

Overall, auto detailing is an important part of vehicle maintenance. Not only does it help to protect your vehicle's exterior and interior, but it also helps to maximize your vehicle's resale value. Whether you're looking to sell your vehicle or simply maintain its aesthetic appeal, regular auto detailing is an important part of vehicle ownership.

When selecting an auto detailer, it's important to choose a reputable auto detailing service that uses quality products and keeps up with the latest and greatest trends in the industry. Cheap products can damage your vehicle's finish and leave it susceptible to damage and premature wear and tear.

When selecting a detailing service, also look for these critical components:

- Offers a warranty or guarantee on their work (as applicable.)
- Delivers customized treatment plans.
- Invests in the latest and greatest technology.
- Utilizes the top performing "lotions and potions" and the most cutting-edge equipment available.

AffluentAutoSpa.com

- Invests in the best training, education, and certifications to increase their team's knowledge, skills, and abilities.

Auto detailing is an important part of your vehicle maintenance and can help extend the life of your vehicle.

Chapter 3

AUTO DETAILING MAY INCREASE YOUR RESALE VALUE

Detailing your vehicle can help to restore its appearance and make it look like new, allowing you to get a higher resale price for it.

> **DETAILING YOUR VEHICLE CAN HELP TO RESTORE ITS APPEARANCE AND MAKE IT LOOK LIKE NEW, ALLOWING YOU TO GET A HIGHER RESALE PRICE FOR IT.**

Other benefits include:

1. Makes your vehicle look new

When you detail your vehicle, it will be rid of any dirt, dust, or grime that has built up on the exterior and interior of the vehicle. Detailing can also restore the paint and make it look new. When potential buyers see a vehicle that looks brand new, they will be more willing to pay a higher price.

Plus, if you plan to keep your vehicle, who doesn't turn an eye to notice it when you drive by?

2. Repair minor imperfections

Detailing can help to repair minor imperfections, such as scratches, paint swirls, and in some cases, chips in the paint. By repairing these types of imperfections, you can make your vehicle look as good as new and increase its resale value.

3. Makes your vehicle more desirable

Auto detailing can make your vehicle more desirable to potential buyers. A detailed vehicle looks clean and well-maintained, which can make it stand out from other vehicles on the market. When a vehicle is clean and well-maintained, buyers will be more likely to pay a higher price.

4. Increases the lifespan of your vehicle

Detailing can also help to increase the lifespan of your vehicle. When you detail your vehicle, you are removing dirt and grime that can cause damage to the paint and other components of your vehicle. By removing this dirt and grime, you can extend the life of your vehicle and make it look like new for longer, which can increase its resale value.

Chapter 4

THE DIFFERENCE BETWEEN CAR WASHING AND AUTO DETAILING

Car washing and auto detailing both involve cleaning the exterior and interior of a vehicle, but they are two very different processes that should not be confused.

Basic car washes can be done at home with a hose or pressure washer, or you can take your vehicle to an automated facility for faster results. An automatic car wash is a quick, convenient way to keep your vehicle looking clean and presentable. It usually involves running your vehicle through an automated machine that uses brushes or cloths to scrub off dirt and grime from the exterior surface of the vehicle, as well as hoses to rinse it off afterward.

The process typically takes around 10 minutes and costs anywhere from $10–$40 depending on where you go. Buyer beware, you get what you pay for. It's important to note, some drive-through car washes use a strong detergent soap to remove the dirt from your vehicle. These detergents/soaps are not PH neutral, which means they can be removing any waxes/sealants that are on your vehicle or

The Difference Between Car Washing and Auto Detailing

diminish ceramic coatings just by driving thru ONE time.

Caution: Automatic car washes (and in some cases, hand-washing) may cause surface scratches or paint swirls which may take away from your vehicle looking its best. The proven way to help prevent swirls and scratches is to apply an advanced ceramic coating. This advanced treatment will protect your vehicle from the elements and help reduce imperfections, all while providing a glossy finish. Plus, it's easy to maintain and surprisingly affordable. If you're looking for a way to keep your vehicle looking its best, vehicle ceramic coating is definitely worth considering.

On the other hand, auto detailing is much more involved than just washing your vehicle's exterior surfaces. It requires meticulous attention to detail in order to make sure every inch of the vehicle is cleaned thoroughly inside and out.

Auto detailing requires a customized "treatment plan" to ensure your vehicle obtains the highest quality outcome for your investment. Detailing involves advanced treatments that

> **AUTO DETAILING REQUIRES A CUSTOMIZED "TREATMENT PLAN" TO ENSURE YOUR VEHICLE OBTAINS THE HIGHEST QUALITY OUTCOME FOR YOUR INVESTMENT.**

remove foreign substances, mineral deposits, and contaminants from your vehicle's paint surface. This is accomplished with advanced processes such as claying, chemical decontamination, polishing, waxing, or ceramic coating.

Detailing may also include vacuuming carpets, steam cleaning, shampooing upholstery, conditioning leather seats (if applicable), waxing paintwork surfaces, polishing chrome trim pieces, etc., all while using specialized tools such as power buffers/polishers in order to achieve maximum shine results without causing damage to delicate surfaces like plastic

The Difference Between Car Washing and Auto Detailing

or rubber trim pieces found around windows/door frames, etc.

Detailing packages vary in cost depending on the quality, cost, and speed of the detailer. For higher-end, more qualified auto detailing companies, your investment can range anywhere from $300 to $2,000+, depending on many vehicle factors such as age, condition, and your preferred outcome, just to name a few.

Also, the price will vary based on the service and protection you're looking for and how extensive it needs to be for each individual job (basic through long-lasting ceramic coatings). Remember, when considering higher-end treatments (i.e.: ceramic coating), do the math based on the number of years you plan to keep the vehicle. For example, a top-of-the-line, five-year full ceramic coating may run $2,000+. Spread that over the five years that you plan to keep the vehicle and it is only $400 a year (which is less expensive than a lower-end wax job every 6 months.)

Although both processes involve cleaning a vehicle's interior and exterior surfaces, car washing is faster and cheaper than auto detailing. However, it does not provide the same outcomes due to its lack of attention to detail and the quality of the products used. Ultimately, each person has their own preference when it comes down to it, a do-it-yourself approach or a done-for-you treatment plan!

Chapter 5

HOW A DO-IT-YOURSELF APPROACH MAY DAMAGE YOUR VEHICLE

We've all heard of electric machines and their potential benefits, but have you ever considered the possible damage they could do to your vehicle? While it may seem like a great idea to use an electric machine for detailing your vehicle, there are several factors that can cause harm if not handled by a certified and fully trained auto detailer.

Electric machines come in various shapes and sizes, from small handheld devices to large professional-grade equipment. These tools are designed for intricate detailing jobs such as polishing paint or sealing surfaces. However, when used incorrectly or without proper training, these powerful machines can easily create more swirls on your paint finishes or ultimately burn through the paint due to improper techniques or excessive pressure applied during operation.

Another major concern when using electric machines is heat buildup caused by friction while polishing or buffing the surface of your vehicle. This can lead to serious paint fading

How a Do-it-Yourself Approach May Damage Your Vehicle

over time and even permanent discoloration in some cases.

If you choose the do-it-yourself path, many professionals recommend avoiding cheap knockoff brands when purchasing electric machines since they tend to lack quality control measures that would ensure optimal performance and safety standards during use on vehicles. Without accessorizing with specific products built specifically for automotive care (which are often more expensive than generic ones), any amateur attempt at using one of these devices might end up being more damaging than beneficial in the long run!

When it comes to your vehicle, you want the best care possible for its paint finish. That is why it's always recommended to entrust this job to an experienced and fully trained auto detailer who can properly handle delicate surfaces without causing any unnecessary damage. A certified auto detailer will have extensive knowledge of vehicle detailing techniques as well as access to specialized tools and products that are designed specifically for automotive care purposes.

> **WHEN IT COMES TO YOUR VEHICLE, YOU WANT THE BEST CARE POSSIBLE FOR ITS PAINT FINISH.**

This ensures optimal results while maintaining safe temperatures during polishing or buffing operations. This is important because many amateurs using electric machines miss the mark due to a lack of proper training and experience!

Moreover, a professional detailer is also familiar with the different types of paint finishes used in modern vehicles so they can adjust their technique accordingly depending on what kind of surface is being worked on (flat/glossy, etc.). With such expertise comes a more detailed approach when taking up tasks like waxing, and applying sealants or ceramic coatings. All of these measures help protect against minor scratches, swirls, or fading caused by improper use of electric machines that could often result in costly repairs down the line.

In short, if you're looking into keeping your vehicle clean, presentable, and protected then make sure you leave this task only in capable hands; otherwise, you might find yourself dealing with more problems than solutions!

Chapter 6

MYTH #1: WASHING YOUR VEHICLE WHEN IT'S DIRTY IS GOOD ENOUGH

Most people wash their vehicles only when there is a noticeable dirt collection, or some kid leaves a "please wash me" message on it. The problem with that "load of dirt" is that foreign substances, mineral deposits, and contaminants eventually start to diminish your wax, and then damage your finish. Avoid this dilemma by establishing an ongoing routine.

People often think they only need to wash their vehicle when it appears dirty. Unfortunately, this could not be further from the truth. The fact is that if you wait until a vehicle has accumulated dirt and grime before washing it, then you are already behind the game. This is because foreign substances like salt and other mineral deposits can start to cause damage to your vehicle's finish even before you notice them on its surface.

The best way to avoid this problem is by establishing an ongoing routine for washing your vehicle. Depending on where you live and how often you drive, this might mean giving your car or truck a thorough wash once a month or every few weeks at least. A better option

Myth #1: Washing Your Vehicle When it's Dirty is Good Enough

> **THE FACT IS THAT IF YOU WAIT UNTIL A VEHICLE HAS ACCUMULATED DIRT AND GRIME BEFORE WASHING IT, THEN YOU ARE ALREADY BEHIND THE GAME.**

may be to enroll in an ongoing, consistent auto detailing maintenance program.

When selecting products for these regular washes, make sure that the soap used is PH-neutral, this will help ensure that you are not stripping away any waxes, sealants, or coatings that have been applied to your vehicle. This will help protect the paint job of your vehicle from UV rays and road contaminants such as oil and grease, which can be particularly damaging over time if left unchecked.

Here are some additional steps to extend your car's finish:

1. After each wash

Use either a silicone-based spray sealant or synthetic polymer detailing spray sealant to provide extra protection against environmental elements such as wind-borne dust particles, ultraviolet radiation (UV) exposure, bird droppings, etc., while also helping repel rainwater off of surfaces more quickly after contact. For vehicles that have ceramic coatings installed, be sure to use a SI02 enhancer about every 3 months for best results.

2. Regularly apply quality waxes/ sealants

Usually yearly, in order to protect both painted surfaces and plastic trim pieces from fading due solely to exposure.

3. Use microfiber cloths

Specifically designed for automotive use instead of paper towels when drying off exterior surfaces after each wash. Microfiber wash mitts are best for an agitation wash, washing the vehicle in straight lines and rinsing the mitt after every panel using the 2-bucket method. DO NOT wash the vehicle in a circular motion, as this is what induces swirl marks in the clear coat.

4. Avoid using harsh abrasives/scrubbing pads

This is important, especially during the cleaning process, since these will strip away protective layers found on top of the clear coat (which act essentially like sunscreen). Doing so may create swirl marks within paintwork that become increasingly visible over time, thus reducing the overall value of the vehicle in terms of resale prices;

By following all of these simple tips, anyone can expect their vehicles to stay looking better longer regardless of whatever location they live in! Moreover, having regularly scheduled maintenance ensures one doesn't fall into the trap many others have done before them, namely leaving dirt build-up, which leads directly towards premature aging, and wear and tear down the road without fail.

In addition to the before mentioned steps for maintaining your vehicle's exterior, there are some possible problems associated with using automatic car washes as well. Many owners mistakenly believe that these machines can clean their vehicles better than they could do themselves and also provide protection from environmental elements such as UV rays.

Unfortunately, this is not always the case since many of these automated systems have powerful brushes which may cause swirls or scratches in paintwork if not used carefully. Furthermore, waxes found inside most automatic washes often don't provide enough protection against UV radiation nor repel

Myth #1: Washing Your Vehicle When it's Dirty is Good Enough

rainwater efficiently so it's best to avoid relying solely on them (when possible).

Therefore when selecting a method for cleaning your vehicle, it's important to ensure you know exactly what type of machine/products will be used beforehand in order to prevent any unnecessary damage from occurring later down the line. Moreover, those who lack time due to busy schedules might consider investing in products like synthetic polymer detailing sprays that offer both convenience and protection at the same time!

Chapter 7

IRONX: THE SECRET INGREDIENT

IronX is an amazing product that helps protect and improve the look of a vehicle's paint finish. It uses advanced technology to break down and remove iron particles from the surface, which can harm its appearance. Professional auto detailers use IronX to not only clean vehicles, but also give them added protection against fading, oxidation, and other environmental conditions.

IronX is an advanced chemical solution created by CarPro USA specifically for removing damaging ferrous (iron) particles from automotive surfaces without causing any damage to the underlying finish or clear coat layer. The product contains active ingredients like hydrofluoric acid (HF), ammonium bifluoride (ABF), propylene glycol monomethyl ether (PGME), surfactants/detergents, corrosion inhibitors, and dyes for color coding when in use.

When applied correctly onto any affected area(s) of your vehicle's exterior or interior surface(s); these components work together to dissolve away oxidized deposits caused by brake dust particles containing metal-based

IronX: The Secret Ingredient

compounds like iron oxide (rust). After being allowed time to dwell on the surface before rinsing off with a water pressure washer or cloth wipe-down method; all contaminants are removed, leaving behind a pristine clean look ready for waxing or polishing treatments afterward if desired by the customer.

When sprayed directly onto contaminated areas of your vehicle's paintwork where there has been exposure to rust/iron contamination, upon contact with air over time, HF reacts with oxygen forming hydrogen fluoride gas which then penetrates deep into pores within metal particles dissolving their base structure, leaving only residue free surface left behind once wiped away.

This process occurs almost instantly, so you don't have to worry about prolonged periods waiting for results as seen in traditional methods like clay bar detailing, which require up to 20 minutes, depending on severity level, before completion. Additionally, due to its specialized formulation design based around specific pH levels designed specifically for automobile detailing applications; no additional pre-cleaning step is needed prior to application, unlike other products available in the market, making a more cost-effective choice compared to competitors while still providing the same great quality results expected trusted brand name like CarPro USA!

Auto detailers know just how important it is to keep vehicles looking their best at all times; thus, they seek out solutions to make sure the job is done right the first time every time, even when faced with tougher cleaning challenges involving embedded iron contaminants, found brake dust, etc.

Traditional methods take longer than needed to complete these tasks leading to unproductive labor hours being wasted, not to mention the risk of potential damage. However, thanks to revolutionary technology now available through CarPro USA's flagship product line, "Iron X" professionals everywhere can quickly get rid of tough dirt debris without fear of harming delicate finishes underneath!

IronX: The Secret Ingredient

Here are some of the additional benefits of using IronX on your vehicle's paint finish:

- Easier & quicker removal of embedded iron contaminates from any type of automotive surface, whether be flat colors, glosses, matte finishes, etc.

- Increased protection against oxidation fading from other environmental conditions.

- Improved overall shine clarity after treatment due to special formulation used during the manufacturing process.

- Cost efficient alternative compared to traditional methods allows professionals to save money while still delivering high-quality services customers expect them to provide!

Using IronX can help preserve a vehicle's aesthetic value and provide extra protection against things like fading and oxidation. Professional auto detailers rely heavily upon

> **USING IRONX CAN HELP PRESERVE A VEHICLE'S AESTHETIC VALUE AND PROVIDE EXTRA PROTECTION AGAINST THINGS LIKE FADING AND OXIDATION.**

this innovative solution because it allows them complete jobs faster than ever before while providing top-notch results every time, so clients leave happily satisfied, knowing their prized possession looks better than ever before.

Chapter 8

ADVANCED CLAY BAR TREATMENT

For many vehicle owners, detailing their vehicles can seem overwhelming. But with the right knowledge and tools, it is simple and rewarding. An important step to achieving a perfect shine on your vehicle's paint job is using an advanced clay bar treatment. This process uses special lubricants and fine abrasive clay to remove dirt or debris from the surface without damaging it.

> **AN IMPORTANT STEP TO ACHIEVING A PERFECT SHINE ON YOUR VEHICLE'S PAINT JOB IS USING AN ADVANCED CLAY BAR TREATMENT.**

So what exactly is this treatment? It is a specialized cleaning method used by professional auto detailers which restore luster to vehicles' surfaces by removing contaminants like road tar, tree sap, industrial fallout, and brake dust from the paintwork.

Advanced Clay Bar Treatment

The basic idea behind this technique is that you start off by applying a lubricant (like detailer wax) where you plan to perform the treatment before taking a soft clay made for automotive use and kneading it until pliable enough for application onto your vehicle's surface. When pressure is applied while rubbing in straight lines, any contaminants stuck within its pores are loosened up and removed without harming the finish.

Once all contaminants have been properly removed using this method, the final polishing/waxing steps would come next. I suggest using high-quality products made especially for these purposes so they don't leave behind residue streaks, marks, etc.

Using an advanced clay bar treatment offers numerous benefits compared to conventional methods such as hand-washing alone. These include longer-lasting shine and depth perception on painted finishes along with better removal rates when dealing with hard deposits, caked deep down into grooves, crevices, etc., versus having difficulty trying to scrub out manually.

Professional auto detailers typically utilize this technique because they know how crucial proper preparation work combined with detailed finishing results leads towards providing the ultimate customer satisfaction levels possible. Investing extra money upfront to have expert professionals carry out advanced clay bar treatments will pay off long-term, both aesthetically and in preserving value.

Chapter 9

PAINT CORRECTION

Vehicles are often seen as a status symbol and a reflection of one's personality. As such, many vehicle owners take great pride in keeping their vehicles looking their best. One way to achieve this is through auto-paint correction. This process can help restore a vehicle's paint to a near-showroom shine and can help preserve a vehicle's value.

Auto paint correction is a process that involves removing surface imperfections, such as scratches, swirl marks, and oxidation, from a vehicle's clear coat. This process is usually done using machine polishers, although some by-hand applicators are available to help with the process. The goal of the process is to

> **AUTO PAINT CORRECTION IS A PROCESS THAT INVOLVES REMOVING SURFACE IMPERFECTIONS, SUCH AS SCRATCHES, SWIRL MARKS, AND OXIDATION, FROM A VEHICLE'S CLEAR COAT.**

Paint Correction

restore the vehicle's paint to its original luster, which can help maintain its value and make it look its best.

When it comes to the process of auto paint correction, the first step is to thoroughly wash the vehicle with a stripping soap. This step is essential to remove any dirt and debris that may be present on the paint. After the vehicle is washed, an iron decontamination and clay bar are then used to remove any embedded contaminants that may be present on the paint. This helps to make sure that the paint is smooth and ready to be polished.

Once the vehicle is prepped and ready, the polishing process can begin. This is typically done with a dual-action or rotary polisher, which works by spinning the polishing pad and applying compound or polish to the paint. The goal of this step is to remove any imperfections and restore the paint to its original shine.

Once the paint is polished, the next step is to wipe the vehicle surfaces down with an IPA (isopropyl alcohol.) The final step is to then protect the paint with a sealant/wax or ceramic coating. This step helps to ensure that the paint remains protected from the elements, such as UV rays and moisture. This step can also help to prevent future oxidation and discoloration.

Auto-paint correction is a great way to restore a vehicle's paint to its original luster. It can help maintain the value of the vehicle and make it look its best. The cost of the process varies depending on the size of the vehicle and the amount of work that needs to be done, but it can be a fraction of the cost of a full paint job. With the right care, auto paint correction can help keep your vehicle looking its best for years to come.

Chapter 10

SURFACE SCRATCHES

Auto detailing is an important part of vehicle care, as it helps to protect your vehicle from the elements and keep it looking its best. One of the most common issues with auto detailing is the removal of surface scratches. While it's possible to repair deeper scratches, surface scratches can usually be removed with the right tools and techniques.

Surface scratches are very shallow scratches that can appear in the clear coat of your vehicle. They usually appear as thin white lines and are caused by contact with a hard object, such as keys or a belt buckle. These scratches are usually too shallow to show up in a car wash, and will only be seen when the vehicle is in direct sunlight or bright light.

> **SURFACE SCRATCHES ARE VERY SHALLOW SCRATCHES THAT CAN APPEAR IN THE CLEAR COAT OF YOUR VEHICLE.**

Surface Scratches

The first step when removing surface scratches from your paint is to clean your vehicle. Start by washing the vehicle with mild car soap and then use a detailing brush to gently scrub the area where the scratches are located. This helps to remove any dirt or debris that may be obscuring the scratches.

Once the area is clean, begin the process of removing the scratches. The first step is to use a clay bar to remove any contaminants from the paint. The clay bar is lightly rubbed in a straight back-and-forth motion over the area and then wiped off with a microfiber cloth.

Next, use an auto detailing polish to remove the scratches. It's important to use a detailing polish specifically designed for vehicles, as regular polishes can cause more damage. Then apply a thin layer of the polish to the scratched area in a circular motion and then wipe off the polish.

Finally, use a wax/sealant to protect the paint from future scratches. This helps to prevent the scratches from reappearing, and will also help to protect the paint from UV rays and other environmental factors.

Removing surface scratches from your vehicle's paint can be a tedious process (and very harmful if not done correctly), but it's important to do in order to keep your vehicle looking its best. When you utilize a fully trained, professional detailer with the right tools and techniques, they can easily remove surface scratches and protect your vehicle from the elements without the risk of damaging your vehicle's finish.

Chapter 11

PAINT SWIRLS VS. NO PAINT SWIRLS

Imagine this . . . As the light reflects off your vehicle's finish, you notice some unsightly paint swirls on your hood. Moving in closer, you discover more paint swirl patterns on the trunk and door panels. You start to get an uneasy and troubled feeling because you realize this is a significant problem.

Every vehicle owner aims to keep their vehicle looking brand new for as long as possible. However, one of the biggest challenges that car owners experience is maintaining their paint. Swirl marks are one of the most annoying issues that many vehicle owners face. The swirls are often caused by improper washing techniques and abrasions during the cleaning process.

Paint Swirls vs. No Paint Swirls

> **SWIRL MARKS ARE ONE OF THE MOST ANNOYING ISSUES THAT MANY VEHICLE OWNERS FACE.**

Paint swirls are those tiny circular scratches that you see on your car's paint. These scratches are caused by many factors, but the most common causes include:

- Washing your vehicle with dirty or abrasive materials.

- Using the wrong towels, such as towels with grit in them.

- Using a car wash that has a spinning brush system.

- Applying too much pressure to the towel while drying.

Essentially, a vehicle with no paint swirls means that the paint is in pristine condition and has not been scratched by abrasive materials or during the cleaning process. Now that we know what paint swirls are and what causes them, let's discuss some tips to avoid paint swirls:

- Always use a two-bucket washing technique to prevent dirt and grit from scratching your vehicle's paint.

- Use the right towels, such as microfiber towels that are specifically designed for car detailing.

- Avoid using a car wash that has a spinning brush system.

- Do not apply too much pressure while drying your vehicle.

- Use a high-quality polish, wax, or ceramic coating to protect your vehicle's paint.

Paint Swirls vs. No Paint Swirls

Vehicle paint swirls are a nuisance to many vehicle owners, and they can be challenging to remove once they occur. The good news is that with the right washing and detailing techniques, you can avoid paint swirls and keep your vehicle looking brand new for years to come. If you're looking for an expert to remove your paint swirls, we suggest you schedule a consultation with a fully trained and certified auto detailer.

Chapter 12

MYTH #2: ELECTRIC MACHINES ARE DAMAGING TO YOUR VEHICLE'S PAINT

Like any high-quality professional service, proper training on the "tools of the trade" is critical. In the wrong hands, a rotary or dual-action polisher could cause more damage than good. Your paint is made to survive some pretty harsh conditions: rain, windstorms, sun, and other elements but those things among others will slowly and continually "beat up" your clear coat. To correct your paint imperfections, you need an experienced detailer with the right equipment.

> **LIKE ANY HIGH-QUALITY PROFESSIONAL SERVICE, PROPER TRAINING ON THE "TOOLS OF THE TRADE" IS CRITICAL.**

The myth that electric machines are damaging to your vehicle's paint is far from reality. In fact, when used properly and with the right equipment, these tools can actually help restore a vehicle's finish to its original beauty. This myth likely stems from people who have

Myth #2: Electric Machines are Damaging to Your Vehicle's Paint

attempted do-it-yourself (DIY) detailing projects without the benefit of proper training or experience. Without this knowledge, an inexperienced detailer could potentially cause more damage than good with a rotary or dual-action polisher.

To understand how modern electric machinery can be beneficial for restoring a vehicle's finish, let's first look at what causes paint imperfections in the first place: UV rays, acid rain, bird droppings, and road salt all slowly break down the protective clear coat on vehicles over time resulting in fading and oxidation of the paint underneath. Addressing these issues requires specialized knowledge and equipment, such as buffers and polishers designed specifically for auto detailing that removes surface contaminants while protecting underlying layers of paintwork.

Unlike traditional abrasive techniques which might leave scratches or swirl marks on delicate surfaces like clear coats, electric machines use advanced microfiber technology to safely remove imperfections from within the vehicle's painted surfaces without causing any harm to the finish. The process works by applying tiny fibers made out of polymers onto automotive paints using either low-speed buffing (for light cleaning) or high-speed polishing (for deeper levels).

Additionally, electric machines come equipped with several safety features including adjustable RPM settings so users can choose between speeds appropriate for each job; built-in heat sensors that detect if temperatures rise beyond safe limits; plus integrated vibration dampening systems which reduce noise pollution during operation making them much less disruptive than their manual counterparts. All these features make professional-grade electric machines ideal solutions for auto detailers looking to restore their customers' cars back to showroom condition without risking permanent damage due to negligence or inexperience.

In summary, when used correctly under supervision from experienced professionals, electric machine tools offer fast efficient methods for removing small blemishes & restoring large

Myth #2: Electric Machines are Damaging to Your Vehicle's Paint

areas of damaged automotive paints back into pristine condition quickly & safely. By following manufacturer instructions closely, operators will be able to achieve remarkable results every time, even on older vehicles whose once beautiful finishes may have been left neglected after years of exposure outdoors. So don't be fooled by myths about damaging effects caused by modern-day power tools, instead recognize them as valuable resources capable of delivering exceptional results faster than ever before when used by a qualified professional.

Chapter 13

MYTH #3: POLISHING ISN'T IMPORTANT IN KEEPING YOUR PAINT LOOKING LIKE NEW

In many cases if polishing is not completed before waxing your vehicle, then you'll notice your paint defects are more visible. Specifically, if your paint is dull, and lifeless, with microscopic scratches and swirls, then polishing your vehicle prior to waxing was probably omitted. Polish is an abrasive product that is used to prepare the paint surface for waxing/sealants (or ceramic coating) by removing paint defects and creating an even surface.

Auto polishing is an important step in maintaining the look and feel of your vehicle's paint. A good auto polish will also help to enhance the shine and luster of your vehicle's finish, which can make it appear newer for longer periods of time.

> **AUTO POLISHING IS AN IMPORTANT STEP IN MAINTAINING THE LOOK AND FEEL OF YOUR VEHICLE'S PAINT.**

Myth #3: Polishing Isn't Important in Keeping Your Paint Looking Like New

When it comes to keeping your vehicle's paint looking like new, nothing beats a professional auto polishing job. Professional detailers often use specialized machines such as orbital buffers to apply polishes evenly over large areas quickly and efficiently with minimal effort.

Polishing can help maintain the color integrity and vibrancy of your vehicle's exterior over longer periods of time. Regularly applying a high-quality car wax after every few washes provides an additional layer of protection against UV rays as well as other environmental elements such as rain, snow, sleet, etc., that may cause fading or discoloration over time if left unchecked. Waxes, sealants, and coatings also add extra glossiness which can bring out even more shine in dark colors like black and navy blue!

Auto polishes are extremely cost-effective solutions, an investment upfront into quality products now means saving money down the road when repairs might otherwise be needed due to damages caused by neglect. This alone should make anyone think twice before skimping out on this essential routine maintenance task, taking care of your vehicle today ensures longevity tomorrow!

Chapter 14

WHAT IS POLISHING AND WHAT ARE THE VARIOUS METHODS?

Having a clean, shiny vehicle is something that many people strive to achieve. However, it takes more than just regular washing and waxing to keep your vehicle's paint looking like new. Polishing your vehicle is an important part of any maintenance routine because it helps protect the paint from damage caused by harsh weather conditions and road debris.

The sun's ultraviolet rays can be extremely damaging to vehicles as they can fade or discolor a vehicle's paint job over time if left unprotected. Polishing with a high-quality wax or sealant will provide a layer of protection against harmful UV rays while keeping your vehicle looking beautiful at all times!

Having a polished vehicle shows that you take pride in its appearance, after all, first impressions count! A well-maintained vehicle speaks volumes about its owner's commitment to upkeep and general care, something that potential buyers may take note of when purchasing used cars in the future!

Overall, regularly polishing your vehicle is essential for preserving its original beauty for

What is Polishing and What are the Various Methods?

> **THE SUN'S ULTRAVIOLET RAYS CAN BE EXTREMELY DAMAGING TO VEHICLES AS THEY CAN FADE OR DISCOLOR A VEHICLE'S PAINT JOB OVER TIME IF LEFT UNPROTECTED.**

years to come; giving you one less thing to worry about maintaining as you drive down life's roads!

There are several different methods of polishing that can be used to maintain the paint job of your vehicle. Machine buffing is one popular option as it uses a rotary or DA (dual action) machine polisher with wax or compound and a soft cloth to remove surface imperfections from the paintwork. This method provides fast results but should always be done by experienced professionals for the best results.

Hand polishing is another great way to bring out the shine in your vehicle's paint job without damaging any underlying layers. You will need a quality foam pad, polish, and cloth along with some elbow grease to get the desired results, though this option can take longer than machine buffing.

Ceramic coatings are becoming increasingly popular due to their long-lasting protection against environmental elements such as sun exposure, water spots, and dirt build-up over time. Ceramic coatings create an extra layer of protection on top of your vehicle's existing finish which can reduce scratches/swirls from occurring while allowing for easy cleaning when needed!

Regardless of what route you choose, regular polishing is essential for preserving the original beauty of your vehicle's paintwork; giving you one less thing to worry about maintaining as you drive down life's roads!

Chapter 15

WHAT IS CERAMIC COATING AND WHY YOU SHOULD HAVE IT APPLIED

AffluentAutoSpa.com

It's important to prep the vehicle surface before applying the ceramic coating. When it comes to protecting your vehicle's paint, there's no better option than vehicle ceramic coating. This advanced protective coating is applied to your vehicle's exterior, giving it a glossy, pristine finish and superior protection against the elements.

> **WHEN IT COMES TO PROTECTING YOUR VEHICLE'S PAINT, THERE'S NO BETTER OPTION THAN VEHICLE CERAMIC COATING.**

Here are a few benefits of vehicle ceramic coatings:

1. Improved appearance

Vehicle ceramic coatings give your vehicle an incredible shine, making it look like it just rolled off the showroom floor.

This coating also helps to reduce swirl marks and other imperfections, making it a great choice for anyone who wants to keep their vehicle looking its best.

2. Longer-lasting protection

Vehicle ceramic coating offers superior protection against the sun's UV rays, road salt, dirt, grime, and other contaminants. This protective barrier helps to keep your vehicle's paint job looking new for longer.

3. Easy maintenance

Auto ceramic coating is easy to maintain. Unlike waxing, which needs to be done frequently, vehicle ceramic coating can last up to 7 years before it needs to be reapplied. This makes it a great choice for anyone who wants to keep their vehicle looking its best without having to spend a lot of time and effort.

4. Great ROI

A vehicle ceramic coating provides a good return on investment, especially when compared to other forms of vehicle paint protection. This makes it a great choice for anyone who wants to keep their vehicle looking its best without breaking the bank.

Vehicle ceramic coating is a great option for anyone who wants to keep their vehicle looking its best. This advanced protective coating offers superior protection from the elements and helps to reduce imperfections, all while providing a glossy finish. Plus, it's easy to maintain and surprisingly affordable. If you're looking for a way to keep your vehicle looking its best for longer, vehicle ceramic coating is definitely worth considering.

Chapter 16

HOW DOES WAXING COMPARE TO CERAMIC COATING?

When it comes to protecting the exterior of your vehicle, there are several options available. Two popular choices for automotive protection are waxing and ceramic coating. Each process has unique benefits and drawbacks, so it is important to consider which one will best suit your needs before investing in either option.

A ceramic coating is a great way to protect your vehicle from the elements and keep it looking its best for years to come. Additionally, it adds a shine that lasts much longer than traditional waxing methods so you don't have to worry about reapplying every few months. In addition, ceramic coatings require minimal maintenance after application compared to waxes which need reapplication every few months. All in all, a professional vehicle ceramic coating is ideal for anyone looking for superior protection and lasting results on their vehicle. Plus, ceramic coatings come with a very long guarantee (3–5+ years and some offer a lifetime guarantee!)

A good wax job is not as good as a professional-grade vehicle ceramic coating

How Does Waxing Compare to Ceramic Coating?

because it does not offer the same level of protection. Wax offers a certain level of protection, but it wears off quickly and needs to be reapplied regularly. A ceramic coating adds an extra layer of protection that helps protect against environmental contaminants such as salt, bird droppings, tree sap, UV rays, and more. It also helps reduce paint fading caused by long-term exposure to sunlight and road debris. The ceramic coating also lasts much longer than a wax job so you don't have to worry about reapplying every few months like with traditional waxing methods.

> **A GOOD WAX JOB IS NOT AS GOOD AS A PROFESSIONAL-GRADE VEHICLE CERAMIC COATING BECAUSE IT DOES NOT OFFER THE SAME LEVEL OF PROTECTION.**

Waxing is a process that involves applying a liquid or paste-like substance onto the paintwork of the vehicle and then buffing off any excess product with a microfiber cloth. This leaves behind an extremely thin layer of protection that acts as a barrier between dirt and dust particles as well as other environmental contaminants, such as bird droppings or tree sap. The downside to waxing is that this layer of protection generally only lasts around four weeks at most before needing reapplication. However, it can provide more immediate results than ceramic coating due to its fast application time and relatively low cost compared to other solutions.

The ceramic coating on the other hand involves applying multiple layers of specialized liquid polymers onto the surface of your vehicle's paintwork followed by curing under heat lamps or using special curing machines for optimal results (UV/Infrared). This creates an incredibly hard protective film over your vehicle's paintwork (upwards of 9H hardness) which provides superior scratch resistance

How Does Waxing Compare to Ceramic Coating?

even when compared to conventional waxes and sealants.

While ceramic coatings require longer application times than traditional waxes, they often last much longer, typically up to two years depending on how well you maintain them. This makes them ideal if you want long-term protection without compromising on shine or luster.

When it comes to protecting the exterior of your vehicle, there are several options available. While do-it-yourself (DIY) waxing and ceramic coating processes can be done at home with decent results, using a professional auto detailing company often provides superior results due to their skilled technicians and access to higher-grade products.

The benefit of using a highly qualified and experienced detailer is that they understand exactly how each product interacts with different surfaces like paintwork or plastic trim pieces; this knowledge allows them to use the right product for each job, ensuring optimal protection for your vehicle. They will also be able to apply the product correctly in order to ensure maximum durability and gloss levels. This is something the do-it-yourself person may not have experience in working with these types of products.

Additionally, many professional auto detailers stock high-quality sealants and waxes that you wouldn't normally find in stores as well as ceramic coatings which offer increased scratch resistance compared to retail solutions. High-quality "lotions and potions" can provide superior long-term protection for your vehicle's finish overall.

Ultimately when deciding whether you should be waxing or using a ceramic coating for your vehicle's exterior depends largely on what kind of performance you're looking for from your chosen product; both processes offer great levels of gloss and depth whilst providing excellent water repellency.

However, if longevity is key then opting for ceramic coatings could be beneficial due to their increased durability over traditional products like carnauba-based waxes and sealants. Ultimately whatever decision you make

How Does Waxing Compare to Ceramic Coating?

regarding automotive care should reflect what works best for you!

Chapter 17

CERAMIC COATING FOR YOUR GLASS

Ceramic coatings are becoming increasingly popular for vehicle owners looking to protect their vehicles from the elements. When applied to glass, such as a vehicle windshield, the ceramic coating may help to protect the glass from scratches, chips, and other damage. It also provides a reflective barrier that helps to reduce glare and UV rays, lowering the amount of energy needed to cool the vehicle's interior.

Additionally, ceramic coatings can help to reduce the visibility of dirt, dust, and other airborne particles, making your vehicle look cleaner for longer. But most importantly, ceramic coating on your vehicle windshield makes perfect sense for safety reasons.

When it comes to your vehicle's windshield, safety should be your number one priority. A cracked windshield can obstruct your vision, making it harder to see oncoming traffic and other potential hazards. It can also be a risk to passengers in the vehicle, as a cracked windshield can shatter. Applying a ceramic coating to your vehicle's windshield is one of the best ways to prevent these issues.

Ceramic Coating for Your Glass

> **WHEN IT COMES TO YOUR VEHICLE'S WINDSHIELD, SAFETY SHOULD BE YOUR NUMBER ONE PRIORITY.**

The ceramic coating acts as an invisible barrier between the windshield and the outside environment, helping to protect the glass from scratches, chips, and other damage. The ceramic coating also helps to reduce the visibility of dirt, dust, and other airborne particles, which can reduce the amount of time you need to spend cleaning your windshield.

In addition to protecting your windshield from damage, the ceramic coating also provides a reflective barrier that helps to reduce glare and UV rays. This is especially beneficial in sunny climates, as the coating helps to keep the vehicle's interior cooler by reflecting the sun's rays. The reduced glare also makes it easier to see oncoming traffic, providing an added layer of safety.

Ceramic coating is also an economical and eco-friendly choice for vehicle owners. The coating is typically applied with a single application and can last for up to five years with proper maintenance. This means you won't need to replace your windshield as often, saving you money on repairs and replacements. The coating also reduces the amount of energy needed to cool the vehicle's interior, helping to reduce your carbon footprint.

Overall, applying a ceramic coating to your vehicle's windshield is an excellent choice for vehicle owners looking to protect their vehicles from the elements. The coating provides a protective barrier that helps to prevent scratches, chips, and other damage, as well as reducing glare and UV rays. Additionally, ceramic coating is an economical and eco-friendly choice, as it can last for up to five years with proper maintenance and reduces the amount of energy needed to cool the vehicle's interior. For these reasons, ceramic coating on your vehicle windshield makes perfect sense.

Chapter 18

WHAT ABOUT INTERIOR DETAILING?

Having your interior detailed is important for many reasons, not just for appearance. In addition to the aesthetic benefits of having a clean and detailed interior, there can also be other health and cleanliness reasons to consider.

The interior of your vehicle is exposed to a variety of allergens, dust, debris, and other contaminants. These can cause respiratory issues for passengers and even for the driver. Having a professional detailing service can help reduce the number of allergens and dust in the vehicle, improving the air quality and reducing the risk of respiratory issues. Additionally, the detailing process will help remove any mold, mildew, and other contaminants that can lead to health problems.

> **THE INTERIOR OF YOUR VEHICLE IS EXPOSED TO A VARIETY OF ALLERGENS, DUST, DEBRIS, AND OTHER CONTAMINANTS.**

What About Interior Detailing?

The interior of your vehicle can get quite dirty over time. Dirt, food, and other debris can build up in the carpets, upholstery, and other surfaces. This can lead to bad odors and a messy appearance. Professional detailing will help remove dirt and debris and leave the interior of your vehicle looking clean and smelling fresh.

Professional detailing will not only improve the appearance of your vehicle, but it will also protect the surfaces from future damage. For example, the detailing process will help protect the leather and upholstery from fading and cracking due to sun exposure and other environmental factors. Additionally, the detailing process will help protect the interior from other damages such as stains and dirt buildup.

Professional detailing will help improve the visibility of your vehicle by cleaning the windows, mirrors, and other surfaces. This can help reduce the risk of accidents and make it easier to see other vehicles on the road.

Interior detailing will not only improve the appearance of your vehicle, but it will also provide health, cleanliness, protection, and safety benefits. When considering auto detailing, make sure to look into the services offered and what they include. Professional detailing services can help make your vehicle look great and keep it running safely and reliably.

Chapter 19

THE IMPORTANCE OF THE RIGHT TRAINING AND EDUCATION

Hiring an auto detailer with the right training and proper certifications is essential to ensure that you receive the highest quality outcome for your vehicles. Auto detailing is a specialized field that requires a deep understanding of the various tools, products, and techniques used to clean, restore, and protect vehicles. A fully trained and certified auto detailer can provide top-notch detailing services and ensure the vehicle looks its best.

> **A FULLY TRAINED AND CERTIFIED AUTO DETAILER CAN PROVIDE TOP-NOTCH DETAILING SERVICES AND ENSURE THE VEHICLE LOOKS ITS BEST.**

They also understand the safety procedures that must be followed in order to protect themselves and their customers. The right training and certifications will also equip the detailer with the knowledge to assess, diagnose and

The Importance of the Right Training and Education

repair any problems that may arise during the detailing process.

You will be more likely to trust a company that hires detailers with the right training and certifications. This will ensure that your vehicle is in good hands and that the work performed is of the highest quality. Furthermore, having a detailer with the right training and certifications may also help that business attract new customers, as a shop that hires certified detailers is likely to be seen as more reliable and professional.

Finally, having the right training and certifications is important for the safety of both the detailer and the vehicle. Detailers must be familiar with the proper safety procedures to ensure that no damage is done to the vehicle during the detailing process. This knowledge will not only protect the vehicle, but it will also protect the detailer from any potential hazards that may arise.

Hiring an auto detailer with the right training and proper certifications is essential in order to provide the best service and protect the reputation of the shop. An auto detailer with the right training and certifications is equipped with the knowledge and skills to properly and safely perform the job. Furthermore, having the right training and certifications is important to protect both the vehicle and the detailer.

Chapter 20

WHAT IS THE INVESTMENT FOR HIGH QUALITY DETAILING?

When it comes to keeping your vehicle looking its best, vehicle detailing can make all the difference. But how much should you actually invest in a vehicle detail? The answer can vary depending on the level of detail you want and the size of your vehicle.

When determining how much you should invest in a vehicle detail, it's important to consider the size of your vehicle, the condition of the exterior and interior, the type of services you're looking for, and the cost of materials and labor.

> **WHEN IT COMES TO KEEPING YOUR VEHICLE LOOKING ITS BEST, VEHICLE DETAILING CAN MAKE ALL THE DIFFERENCE.**

What is the Investment for High Quality Detailing?

You should consider these factors when investing in a high quality detailing service:

1. Size of your vehicle

One of the most important factors to consider when determining how much you should invest on a vehicle detail is the size of your vehicle. Generally, the larger the vehicle, the more expensive the detail will be. This is because more materials and labor will be required to properly clean and protect the entire vehicle.

For example, a larger SUV or truck may require more time and effort to properly clean and protect all surfaces. On the other hand, a smaller sedan may be easier to clean and detail in less time, resulting in a lower cost.

2. Condition of the exterior and interior

The condition of the exterior and interior of your vehicle is also an important factor to consider when determining how much you should invest in a vehicle detail. If your vehicle is in relatively good condition, you may be able to get away with a basic detail that includes a wash and wax, interior vacuum and wipe down, and glass cleaning.

On the other hand, if your vehicle is in poor condition, then you may need to invest in a more comprehensive detailing package that includes a thorough cleaning and detailing of both the interior and exterior of the vehicle. This will likely cost more, as it requires more time and effort to properly restore your vehicle to its original condition.

3. Type of services

The type of services you're looking for will also affect how much you should invest on a vehicle detail. If you're just looking for a basic wash and wax, then you may be able to get away with investing less. However, if you're looking for more in-depth services such as paint correction or ceramic coating, then you should expect to invest more.

What is the Investment for High Quality Detailing?

4. Cost of materials and labor

The cost of materials and labor is another important factor to consider when determining how much you should invest in a vehicle detail. The cost of materials will depend on the type of products used and the quantity needed for the job. The cost of labor will depend on the experience and skill of the detailer, as well as the time it takes to complete the job.

5. Your investment

On a basic detail, you should expect to invest anywhere from $250 to $500+. This may include:

- Full interior detail excluding shampoo/steam cleaning.

- Exterior detail, 2x wash with a foam cannon and wash mitts.

- Includes door jambs cleaned, wheels, tires, and fenders cleaned/dressed.

- Clay barring treatment.

- Approximate 6-month paint sealant.

- Wax treatment.

For an intermediate detailing package, you can expect to invest between $500 to $750+. This may include the same components as the package above but will likely include at least a 12-month sealant.

For the most comprehensive (and cost-effective) detailing packages that include paint correction, ceramic coating, full interior cleaning, and other advanced treatment plans, you should expect to invest between $750 to $2,500+.

The cost of a vehicle detail can vary depending on the size of your vehicle, the condition of the exterior and interior, the type of services you're looking for, and the cost of materials and labor.

Chapter 21

THE BENEFITS OF MOBILE AUTO DETAILING

Auto detailing is a specialized service that involves a deep cleaning, polishing, and waxing of a vehicle's exterior and interior surfaces. It is a great way to restore a vehicle's original beauty and can even increase its value. But, depending on where you live, it can be difficult to access a quality auto detailing service. That's why many people are now turning to mobile detailers to bring the auto detailing experience to their doorstep.

Mobile detailing benefits include:

1. Convenience

The biggest benefit of mobile detailers is the convenience they offer. You simply schedule a consultation, set up the treatment plan and they take it from there. You don't have to travel to the detailer's shop, or waste time waiting in line. All you have to do is call the detailer, and they will come to your home on a day and time that is convenient for you. This eliminates the hassle of having to transport your vehicle to and from the shop. You

The Benefits of Mobile Auto Detailing

can even have the detailer come to your workplace if that is more convenient for you.

2. More time

Another great advantage of mobile detailers is that they save you time. When you take your vehicle to a shop for detailing, you generally have to wait for them to finish the job. This can take several hours, or even days, depending on the work that needs to be done. With a mobile detailer, the job is usually done in just a few hours.

3. Higher quality outcomes

Mobile detailers are often more experienced than shop-based detailers, and they're able to provide higher quality work. This is because they have more time to focus on your vehicle, and they don't have to rush to finish it. They are also able to provide more personalized service, as they are able to talk to you directly to understand your needs and preferences.

AffluentAutoSpa.com

4. Cost-effective

Mobile detailers are often more cost-effective than shop-based detailers. This is because they don't have to pay for overhead costs, such as rent, utilities, and staff that shop-based detailers have to pay for. This means that they can charge lower rates, which in turn can save you money.

5. What to look for

When looking for a company that provides auto detailing services, there are a few things you should look for:

- **Experience**—You want to make sure that the company you hire has experience in auto detailing. Ask them how long they have been in business, and what kind of experience they have.

- **Reputation**—You should also take the time to research the company's reputation. Check online

The Benefits of Mobile Auto Detailing

reviews to see what other people have to say about their services.

- **Quality**—Make sure that the company uses high-quality products and tools. This will ensure that your vehicle looks its best when the job is done.

- **Insurance**—A reputable auto detailing company should have insurance to protect you and your vehicle. This is important in case something goes wrong during the detailing process.

- **Price (Investment)**—Make sure that the company you hire is offering a competitive price. You should be able to find a company that offers quality services at a reasonable price.

Auto detailing is a great way to restore your vehicle's original beauty and increase its value. With the convenience and cost-effectiveness of mobile detailers, you can now enjoy the benefits of auto detailing without ever leaving your home. To get the most out of your auto detailing experience, make sure to research the company you hire, and look for one that has the experience, a good reputation, quality products and tools, and the proper insurance. With the right auto detailing company, you can have a beautiful, well-maintained vehicle that you can be proud of.

> **WITH THE CONVENIENCE AND COST-EFFECTIVENESS OF MOBILE DETAILERS, YOU CAN NOW ENJOY THE BENEFITS OF AUTO DETAILING WITHOUT EVER LEAVING YOUR HOME.**

Chapter 22

WHY AUTO ENTHUSIASTS CHOOSE A DETAILING MAINTENANCE PROGRAM

AffluentAutoSpa.com

Are you an auto enthusiast looking for a way to take your vehicle's appearance to the next level? If so, then you should consider investing in an ongoing VIP detailing maintenance program. An ongoing maintenance detailing program can offer a number of benefits that can help you keep your vehicle in top condition and make it look its best.

> **AN ONGOING MAINTENANCE DETAILING PROGRAM CAN OFFER A NUMBER OF BENEFITS THAT CAN HELP YOU KEEP YOUR VEHICLE IN TOP CONDITION AND MAKE IT LOOK ITS BEST.**

Here are the benefits of an ongoing auto detailing maintenance program:

1. Longer lifespan

An ongoing maintenance detailing program can help extend the life of your vehicle. This is because regular cleaning and detailing will help protect the vehicle's body, paint, and interior from fading, rusting, and other damage caused by the elements.

2. Improved appearance

Detailing your vehicle on a regular basis will help it look brand new. Your vehicle's paint will be gleaming and its interior will be spotless. An ongoing maintenance detailing program will also help preserve the value of your vehicle in case you decide to sell it in the future.

3. Cost savings

Investing in an ongoing maintenance detailing program can actually save you money in the long run. This is because the cost of the detailing services will be much lower than the cost of repairs or replacements for any damage that occurs due to a lack of maintenance.

Overall, an ongoing maintenance detailing program can be a great investment for a car enthusiast. Not only will it help keep your vehicle in top condition, but it can also help protect your vehicle's value and extend its lifespan. Investing in an ongoing maintenance detailing program is a great way to make sure that your vehicle looks good and lasts longer.

An ongoing maintenance detailing program is critical for protection against the harsh elements of the environment. In addition, protecting your vehicle from the sun, heavy rain, tree and bird droppings, rain spot etching, and debris contamination is critical. We'd like to invite you to participate in our Affluent Auto Spa VIP monthly detailing service that provides additional protection and keeps your vehicle looking its best all year round.

We created this program to preserve your vehicle and we highly recommend it because your vehicle will remain clean, protected, and just look amazing.

Because you have this book, you're entitled to a significant discount on this ongoing service.

Why Auto Enthusiasts Choose a Detailing Maintenance Program

There is no contract, it's an easy month-to-month agreement. We'll send you a reminder each month to schedule a convenient time for your service. So you'll stay ahead of the dirt and grime and ensure your vehicle stays in tip-top condition. As an Affluent Auto Spa VIP member, you'll also receive online priority scheduling and preferential treatment.

Remember "maintenance is better than the cure." As a member of this exclusive program, dirt, and grime are not allowed to sit for long periods of time and therefore do not damage your vehicle's finish.

In addition, our VIP maintenance detail can:

- Extend the life of products that we already applied to your vehicle.

- Help avoid more expensive in-depth cleaning requirements due to long-term contaminants on your vehicle.

- Greatly enhance your appreciation and enjoyment of your vehicle.

This VIP service includes:

- Hand washing your vehicle's exterior and decontaminating the paint surface (if needed.)
- Cleaning the wheels and tires.
- Light vacuuming of your interior.
- Wiping down your interior surfaces and applying a low gloss UV protectant to the surfaces.
- Cleaning your interior glass (if needed.)
- Applying spray wax to your paint surface to extend paint sealant life (if necessary.)
- Applying tire dressing to your tires.

Why Auto Enthusiasts Choose a Detailing Maintenance Program

Call/Text **(210) 679-1472**

Pickup/delivery service available for non-mobile treatments

Licensed + Insured

To learn more, go to **AffluentAutoSpa.com/VIPMO** right now.

TO LEARN MORE, GO TO AFFLUENTAUTOSPA.COM/VIPMO RIGHT NOW.

AffluentAutoSpa.com

We are looking forward to servicing your vehicle. So let's get you going right now! No contracts, no hassle, no worries, just you having a great-looking vehicle all year long!

Chapter 23

WHAT CLIENTS, JUST LIKE YOU, ARE SAYING ABOUT THE AFFLUENT AUTO SPA

AffluentAutoSpa.com

Reserve Your Vehicle Consultation-Estimate Now. It's so Easy and Convenient Because We Come to You!

AffluentAutoSpa.com

Call/Text **(210) 679-1472**

Pickup/delivery service available for non-mobile treatments

Licensed + Insured

What Clients, Just Like You, are Saying About the Affluent Auto Spa

Easy and Convenient

"I was especially happy that they offer the mobile service. My car was detailed as I worked and had no inconvenience of having to take it somewhere, very easy!"

—Rebekah Hawes ★★★★★

Done Fast and Done Correctly

"The treatment was done fast and correctly. The ceramic coating turned out fantastic! He even took care of some small scratches I had that were pre-existing!"

—Drake Davis ★★★★★

The Right Knowledge, Tools, and Equipment

"Amazing, professional, and knowledgeable company. Took the time to come out and get myself set up with the best option that suited me. My vehicle is wrapped and they had the right knowledge, tools, and equipment to work on my car!"

—Matthew Villarreal ★★★★★

Beautiful Ceramic Coating!

"Dylan came highly recommended for ceramic coating and did not disappoint. He did a fabulous job! He was very professional and detailed about the service from start to finish. This was the best anniversary gift I could give my husband, he loves it! 5-year ceramic coating by the Affluent Auto Spa is the way to go, don't go anywhere else! Affluent comes to you and does an outstanding job. Thank you so much, Dylan!"

—Becky Majors ★★★★★

Just Magic!

"The service provided is astounding. I had the badges removed from my vehicle and the #2 treatment plan. The work was done meticulously and thoroughly. There is absolutely zero evidence that the badges were ever there. The paint underneath is beautiful. The car looks incredible and I couldn't be happier. Thanks again for your incredible work and effort!"

—Sam Beckett ★★★★★

Very Impressed!

"I was super impressed to see the finished product of my car! We had gone to the beach and we have a baby, but looking at my car you'd think it was brand new! Not only was everything done super well, but Dylan is so fast! I will definitely be using Affluent Auto Spa again and recommending them to everyone! Thanks, Dylan."

—Jess Gonzalez ★★★★★

The Only Guy I Trust With My Cars!

"Dylan has been phenomenal with all of my vehicles. Service, quality, value, and professionalism have always been on par. I trust that I can leave him my vehicle and return to find showroom-worthy paint when I return. Any friends and family I've referred to him have turned into repeat customers for a reason. Dylan is the man!"

—Anthony Kuri ★★★★★

CLEAN FREAK Perfection!

"I had never had any of my vehicles detailed. I clean them all the time myself and keep everything in great shape. The only thing I never really thought about was the paint. Before starting the treatment, Dylan showed me the scratches and swirls all over my car. After polishing and applying the ceramic coating, they ALL disappeared, I was so thrilled! The paint is just POPPING now! I feel so pleased with his work and detail towards my prized possessions."

—Vicki O'Meara ★★★★★

Wonderful Gift—Happy Wife!

"Gave the gift of detailing to my wife for Valentine's Day and it did not disappoint! Dylan did an amazing job and his customer service is exceptional. What I really appreciated was his thorough explanation of the products he used and their quality versus others on the market. He was punctual and his communication was excellent throughout the entire experience. His equipment is top of the line and the end result was 5 stars! Thank you AffluentAutoSpa!"

—Chris Fierro ★★★★★

The Entire Process was Efficient and Easy!

"I'm so happy with how my car looks! The whole process from booking to the actual detail was efficient and easy. Amazing service! Worth every penny!"

—Alex Trey ★★★★★

Awesome Service + Outstanding Work!

"Affluent Auto Spa was so easy to work with, I booked my time for 2 vehicles, and they showed up when they said they would and got right to work. Our vehicles look absolutely clean and sleek. On a scale of 1–10, I give them a 10+! Punctual, fast, detailed, great pricing, and friendly. Give them a call for detailing right at your own home or business!"

—Linda Coffman ★★★★★

Awesome Job!

"Great job on cleaning the interior of my truck and the wax job on the Range Rover. Looks better than new!"

—Bob Johnson ★★★★★

Can't Fake This Shine!

"Affluent is hands down the best detail I have ever had on my vehicle. This company is top-notch and knows auto detailing. Their work speaks for itself. Called up AAS and set up an appointment to get my truck detailed at the last minute, they worked with me to get me on the schedule and even showed up ahead of time. I have used many other companies in the past, but I can say this company has blown me away! I don't think my truck has looked this good inside and out since it was new. Not only is their work top-notch, but they are very professional as well. This is the only company I will trust moving forward to care for my vehicles. Definitely will be recommending them to anyone and everyone. Thank y'all again for such a great shine!"

—Erick Boan ★★★★★

Awesome!

"I could not be more pleased with the absolutely beautiful result that Dylan and Kolby did on my vintage 1950 Ford Deluxe Convertible. You can see yourself in much depth in the finish now as if you could dive into it. Their attention to detail and their professionalism are excellent. They showed up right on time and could not have been nicer or done a better job. I recommend them wholeheartedly!"

—Barry ★★★★★

Top Notch Work!

"Dylan came and fully protected my new truck shortly after bringing it home from the dealership. I thought the truck looked great

AffluentAutoSpa.com

when I purchased it, but Dylan had my truck looking even better after a full exterior detail, ceramic coating, and interior detail. Great work and scheduling was a breeze! I would highly recommend Dylan and Affluent Auto Spa for any of your detailing needs."

—Zack Norman ★★★★★

Good as New!

"After Dylan worked on my car it looked like it was brand new! I am so pleased at how nice and shiny my car looks. The two-year coating he applied removed all the marks and swirls that had been visible for years. This is for sure the best job I have ever seen done on my car, thanks, Dylan and team!"

—Ze'ev Bar-Yadin ★★★★★

Best in the Business!

"Dylan, the owner, was extremely professional, very humble, and generous when it came to my mess of a car. I was really worried nothing could be done about it but Dylan took *his time to make sure the proper care was given. It took a little longer than he anticipated (I figured it would from the get-go). He kept me up to date throughout the entire treatment by sending me photo updates on where he was at and what was going on. Will 100% be back and glad I came in contact with him through a prior customer's referral."*

—Raf Nigaglioni ★★★★★

Top Notch Service!

"When I contacted Dylan, I wanted a full detail on my truck. I expected he would have the vehicle for at least 2 days. He picked up the truck in the morning and had it back to me the same day! I was thoroughly impressed with the final outcome. My truck had tons of scratches and swirls on it from the ranch. My black truck came back with a mirror finish, worth every penny. I would recommend this company to anyone."

—Paul Colavecchia ★★★★★

Dylan Does Amazing Work!

"I had Dylan detail the inside of my car after my birthday, and it looked even better than the day I picked it up from my dealership. Very accommodating when it comes to your conveniences. Thank you again!"

—Sophia Catinella ★★★★★

Notes

Notes

Notes

Notes

Notes

www.ingramcontent.com/pod-product-compliance
Lightning Source LLC
Chambersburg PA
CBHW062059290426
44110CB00022B/2650